BIBLE STUDY FOR ATHEISTS, AGNOSTICS, AND FREETHINKERS

BIBLE STUDY FOR ATHEISTS, AGNOSTICS, AND FREETHINKERS

Gott and Licht

Quiet Waters Publications

2024

Quiet Waters Publications

http://www.quietwaterspub.com

ISBN 978-1-962698-06-1

This priceless first-century cameo was created to celebrate the transfer of power from Emperor Caligula to Emperor Claudius on January 25, 41. But the designer and final editor made the mistake of humiliating one of the men.

The Empress gives the middle-finger[1] to the man who sits below her, head bowed, dejected and seemingly defeated. The flaunting of this gesture—preserving it in stone—may have provoked him to rebel against the Empress, join the opposition, and destroy everything the Julio-Claudians had tried to do for the women of the Empire.

INTRODUCTION

Many of the known circumstances that led to the creation of the first Hebrew Bible have been overlooked or intentionally ignored. Consequently, the existence of a valid, rational interpretation is unknown, leaving superstition-filled interpretations to flourish.

Concurrent with the Babylonian Captivity of Jewish priests and scribes (c. 587–c. 515 BCE), the Greek scholar Pythagoras traveled around the known world, studying and documenting oral and written histories and traditions of major civilizations.

Iamblichus (c. 245–c. 325 CE) was a Neoplatonist biographer who provides most of what is known about Pythagoras. Iamblichus reports that Pythagoras visited the Nazarenes at Mount Carmel before traveling to Egypt where he conducted "most studious research."

He "acquired wisdom" from Egyptian priests, observed mystery rituals, and studied astronomy and geometry. After twenty-two years he was taken to Babylon where "the Magi instructed him in their venerable knowledge," including arithmetic, music, and "other sciences." He remained in Babylon twelve years.[2]

Is it only a coincidence that Pythagoras was in Babylon twelve years—with the material collected while conducting his research—during the latter years of the Babylonian Captivity—when the first version of the Old Testament doctrines was compiled and edited then delivered to Jerusalem?[3]

Is it only a coincidence that a new version of Hebrew script emerged with this first edition of Old Testament doctrines?[4]

Greek historian Plutarch[5] offers a clue to the origins of this new script as he confirms Pythagoras' knowledge of, and respect for, Egyptian priests:

"Pythagoras, it seems, was greatly admired, and he also greatly admired the Egyptian priests, and, copying their *symbolism and occult teachings, incorporated his doctrines in enigmas"*[6] (emphasis added).

A generation before Plutarch, Philo of Alexandria[7] whom Clement of Alexandria[8] referred to as "The Pythagorean,"[9] revealed what can now be seen as "The Key" to solving the "occult teachings" of Hebrew Bible doctrines (See Appendix).

Late Biblical Hebrew is comprised of consonants—no vowels, no spaces, no punctuation. These elements are chosen based on the words needed to convey the story being told.

Judean scribes chose vowels and spaces to fulfil their duty to promote a *male-superiority agenda*. Essene-Nazarene scribes chose vowels and spaces to fulfil their duty to promote an *egalitarian agenda*.

This inspired consonant-only script allows a scribe to imbed an "occult teaching" into a widely-accepted but opposing text. Examples of this ingenious feature are the basis of this work.

It's important to note—and important to remember—that the *rules for interpreting Biblical Hebrew* are not to be confused with the ancient *rules for solving enigmas in the Hebrew Bible.* Different goals, different rules.

Long before Pythagoras gathered the world's knowledge, traditions, and secret teachings and delivered them to Babylon, kings and queens sold themselves as descendants of gods and goddesses. As such, they assumed some form of their deity's name.

King Nebuchadnezzar's deity was *Nebu/Nabu. Nebuchadnezzar* is from the Akkadian words *Nabu* ("father An"), *kudurru* ("eldest son"), *naṣāru* ("protect"). Nebuchadnezzar was the Babylonian king who conquered Jerusalem and relocated YHWH's obstinate priests and scribes to Babylon for re-education and indoctrination.[10]

Nasaru/nasar/nazar can be associated with a word scattered throughout the Bible, beginning with Joseph a NZR (*NeZiR*; Gen 49:26) and concluding with "Jesus *the Nazarene.*"

NaZaR identifies "one who protects" (Akkadian); in Hebrew NZR (*NaZaR/NeZeR/NeZiR*) is defined as "to

6

dedicate, consecrate, crown, separate."[11] NZR is employed in the Hebrew Bible to identify a dynasty of kings and queens, referred to individually as *LHM*.

Alexander the Great was the first to attempt to convert *Orthodox Jews* to *Hellenistic Judaism*.[12] He commissioned a Greek translation of the Hebrew Bible the *Septuagint*.[13] This effort resulted in Jewish kings and queens naming their children *Alexander* and *Alexandra*.

Rome's second attempt to convert Jews was the Maccabean revolt that saw Hellenized[14] and Orthodox Jews engage in a religious war, a continuation of Old Testament conflicts between YHWH and his most hated adversaries, Baal and Asherah.

The Hellenist Hasmoneans (the Maccabee family) prevailed, and a queen, Salome Alexandra, ruled the Jews from c. 76 – 67 BCE following the death of her husband, King Alexander Jannaeus (c. 103 – 76 BCE).[15]

By the time of Jesus the Nazarene, Jews in and out of Jerusalem were familiar with the Septuagint, and many Greek-speaking orthodox Jews converted to Christianity because of the way it was interpreted to them. In response, Jewish priests declared the

Septuagint to be full of lies. The only true scriptures, they argued, were written in Hebrew.[16]

Between the sixth and eleventh centuries, a group of Jewish scribes, the *Masoretes*, became the predominant source for translations, and the majority of English translations and interpretations are based on the *Masorete Text*.[17]

The Bible interpretation that is the source of this study has been available since the first Bible was etched on scrolls in Babylon. But the key to opening it is a system of rules that have been withheld. The Bible carries everything needed to definitively answer a plethora of biblical questions including the *Big One*:

Jesus the Nazarene: historical or mythological?

CHAPTER ONE

EVE AND ADAM

Genesis 1:1 opens with the introduction of *Elohim*, **plural** for the word translated "God," a fact ignored by Jews and Christians.

This mistranslation has been ignored because *Elohim* refers to *two* people: a king identified in scripture as *Eloah* (trans. "God") and a queen identified as *LHM, El ha Em* (trans. "God the Mother"). She and/or they appear 2,598 times in the Old Testament.

Biblical Hebrew provides no word for "goddess" other than naming the demonized foreign goddesses, *Asherah*[18] and *Ashtarot*.[19] However, reconstructing a Hebrew word for "goddess" can be accomplished with simple logic: If Hebrew for "man" is *iSh* and "woman" is *iShasha*, then "God," is *El* and "Goddess" is *Ela*.

Genesis 1:2-25 describe the couple, *Elohim*, working to establish an environment conducive to sustaining life—without hunting and gathering—culminating with *bara*[20] ("*creating*" or "*choosing*") *Adam* (a *zakar,* trans. "male")[21] and a *neqab* (trans. "female").[22]

The Adam's rib version is recited only *after* Gen 2:4 introduces a second king, identified as *YHWH* (trans. "LORD").

YHWH teams up with El and Ela Ha Em to become *YHWH-LHM*, a partnership that ends when King Yahweh escorts a disobedient Adam out of the Garden of Eden.

YHWH-LHM are loosely tied to gods and goddesses introduced in the *Enuma Elis*,[23] a Babylonian creation myth written on clay tablets and generally dated between c. 1700 BCE – 2000 BCE. This earlier story features An-sar and Ki-sar and their royal sons and daughter, Enki-Ea, En-lil, and Nin-lil.

Ansar (NSR) can also be rendered NaSaR, the possible etymology for Nasar/Nazar-ene). Ki-sar can also be written *Kaisar* and *Caesar*.

Sar in a name identifies daughters and sons of most-high royalty—"gods and goddesses." Julius Caesar (Kisar/Kaisar) claimed descent from Venus. Perhaps he knew of legends that suggested to him that Ansar and Kisar came to Earth from the planet Venus.[24]

A careful examination of the Hebrew words in Genesis 2:7 reveal a rational explanation for the biblical story of creation:

"(Yahweh, El, and Ela Ha Em) *yatsar adam aphar min adamah...*"

The Hebrew word *yatsar*[25] is from *tsarar*[26] which can be translated, "to bind, tie up, oppress." In other words, they captured and restrained the Adam.

The Hebrew word PR—*aPhaR* (trans. "dust") can also be rendered PeRi[27] (trans. "fruitful") and *PeRa*[28] (trans. "long-haired"), an equally valid rendering and a better choice for the sociocultural anthropologist.

Adamah[29] is translated "ground."

"Hairy cave-dwellers that lived underground," whose *likeness* resembled the King and Queen, is a description of the species, *Neanderthal*, known to coexist with the earliest European Homo sapiens, *Cro-Magnon*, aka, *Humans.* When the Cro-Magnons established settlements and began farming and domesticating animals, Neanderthals continued hunting and gathering.[30]

Genesis describes a eugenics program envisioned to improve the captured *Adams* by mating them with females of higher intelligence. To produce these superior females, the Kings—Yahweh and El—impregnate a neqab, resulting in *chavvah,*[31] aka, "Eve" (trans. "life-giver").

The *Eves* were hybrids "created" to give life to a new improved species. Falling intellectually between Cro-Magnon and Neanderthal, the hybrid daughters of Yahweh and El are called *Ishshah;*[32] their sons are called *Ish.*[33]

"Adam *yada*[34] Eve his wife and she conceived and bore Cain (Qayin)" (Gen 4:1). It has been assumed that "yada," translated "knew," means they mated. But *yada* could also mean that Adam had previously met Eve; a similar word, *yadah,* is translated "praise."[35]

Eve's words following Cain's birth correct the misconception that Adam impregnated her: "I have *qaniti*[36] *("acquired")* an *Ish*[37] *from Yahweh."* Eve identifies King Yahweh as the biological father of her first-born son. This lineage became the *Tribe of Yah dah* (trans. "Praise YHWH"), known today as *The Tribe of Judah.*

Notably, El and Ela ha Em did not participate in this "acquisition" of Eve's first-born son. However, her second son's name suggests El's significant participation: *Ab El* is translated "Father Eloah."

El's son with Eve did not till the land; Abel was "a shepherd of the tson,"[38] (trans. small cattle, sheep, goats, flock; Gen. 4:2). The offspring of Eve and El became the *Tribe of Israel*, from *Ishshah or El* (trans. "Man/Woman Light Eloah").

YHWH and LHM give the Adams permission to partake from every tree **except** the "tree of knowledge of good and evil," and they warn that he will die if he disobeys (Gen 2:15).

Several valid words can be created when an *S* appears in a string of consonants. At Gen 2:9, *tree* in "the tree of life" and *tree* in "the tree of knowledge of good and evil" are written, *eS*. The Hebrew word for *fire* is also *eS*.[39] The word for *man* is *iS*.

13

The word for *soul* is *neph-eSh*)[40]; therefore *eS, tree* or *fire*, represents beings with a soul. The highest-class—kings and queens—were nazar[41] *or nezer.*[42] Just below them are the king's and queen's siblings, nieces, and nephews—who serve as priests, priestesses, and teachers—"the tree of knowledge of good and evil."

Both royal classes carried the *eS* that identifies *conscience*—knowing right from wrong—perhaps carried in mitochondrial DNA passed on by queens, the *Esh-enes/Essenes.* If so, it would not be present in Eve's or her descendants' DNA.

The text is not about trees; it's about men and women with *eS*, the essence of the fully-human beings that was not recognized in cave-dwellers.

The remaining inhabitants of the garden were ranked beneath the royal family: the "upper class" (merchants and scribes); the "lower class" (laborers and artisans), and subservient slaves. The domesticated Adams were given permission to mate with them, but not with royal women.

The Neanderthal males were threatened with death if they impregnated a royal woman; however, their animal-sexual drive was apparently not satiated with an unlimited number of non-royal females. At least one impregnated a member of the royal family. The result of this transgression is described at Gen 3:22-3:

"And Yahweh-Elohim said 'Behold the Adam has become as one of us to know good and evil and now lest he put forth his hand and take also of the tree of life and eat and live forever'—therefore Yahweh-Elohim sent him forth from the garden of Eden to till the ground..."

To protect and preserve the eS exclusive to queens and their daughters, the Adams—along with the Eves' hybrid children with Yahweh and El—are sent away, ruled by Yahweh and assigned to till the ground and tend to the animals.

Without compassion and judgment to guide them, survival of the fittest was their way of life and a threat to successful settlements. The solution was to instill fear and inflict punishments to tame and to train them. The Ten Commandments with violations punishable by death solved the problem.

El and LHM's daughters and sons remained in the Garden to populate Earth with self-aware beings who respond to compassion and reason—the philosophers and teachers; the innovators and visionaries—who could analyze surroundings, improve technology, and advance foundations that sustain and enhance life on Earth.

"And when (Jesus *the Nazarene*) was alone, those who were with him with the twelve asked him concerning the parables. 'And he said to them, 'To you has been given the *secret of the Kingdom of LHM*, but for those outside, everything is in parables, so that they may indeed see but not perceive, and may indeed hear, but not understand...'" (Mark 4:10, emphasis added).

Pythagoras introduced an enigmatic system of writing—*Late Biblical Hebrew*. The embedded secrets can be retrieved only by those who are given the key— "ears to hear." This lexical innovation first appears at Gen 1:1 which opens with the Hebrew consonants

BRSTBRLHM.

Judeans and Israelites add vowels and spaces to render these consonants,

BaReSiT BaRa eLoHiM...

"In the beginning created Gods..."

Essene-Nazarenes render the same consonants,

BaR iSh eT aB oR eLa Ha eM...

"Son of Man and Father Light Goddess the Mother..."
the original *Holy Trinity.*

Goddess the Mothers and their daughters were required to mate with god-kings (uncles, cousins, step-brothers, half-brothers).

The town of *Bethlehem* (BTLHM) solves several riddles. In addition to *BeT LeHeM* (trans. "house of bread"), BTLHM can be rendered *BaT eLa Ha eM* (trans. "Daughter Goddess the Mother") and *BeTuLaH eM* (trans. "Virgin Mother"). Isn't that amazing?!

In the Hebrew Bible, *Virgin Mothers* are queens and their daughters who produced sons and daughters with kings.

The "abomination" in Leviticus 18:22 refers to a *zakar* impregnating Judean and Israelite women: "And a *zakar* shall not lie with *ishshah*; it is an abomination." The Adams were *zakar*, Neanderthal males who produced physically similar but intellectually inferior offspring. Leviticus has nothing to do with homosexuality.

Leviticus describes the proscriptions imposed when Neanderthal males became a liability, leading to their eventual extinction. But their DNA was passed on through subsequent generations, and an average of 2 percent remains in modern humans.

A sliding scale of surviving traits range from favoring authoritarian dictators to favoring egalitarian humanists—with infinite degrees of passion.

Acknowledging and respecting the natural evolution of our ancestors' eugenics experiment could lead to a mutually beneficial coexistence. Jesus the Nazarene pointed to *The Way* with this summary of his teachings (Luke 6:31):

Treat others the same way you want them to treat you.

Peaceful coexistence is possible, but only if His teachings are practiced—and if all opinions of who and what He is are respected: "God"; "Son of God"; "Savior"; "Son of God and Goddess"; "Teacher"; "Prince of Peace," or "wise man." Choose what makes sense and feels right, but of those professing other faiths, Jesus said (Luke 6:37),

"Do not judge, and you will not be judged. Do not condemn, and you will not be condemned. Forgive, and you will be forgiven.

CHAPTER TWO

SARAH AND ABRAHAM

King YHWH calls Sarah, *Sarai*[43] (trans. "Princess"); he calls Abraham *Abram* (trans. "Father exulted").[44] Abram built an altar to King YHWH east of *Beit el* (trans. "House of Eloah").

> "YHWH said to Abram, 'Go from your country and your kindred and your father's house to the land that I will show you. And I will make of you a great nation...I will bless those who bless you, and him who curses you I will curse; and by you all the families of the earth shall bless themselves'" (Gen 12:1-3).

But what follows seems more a curse than a blessing. A great famine forces Abram and Sarai to relocate to

Egypt. As they approach Pharaoh's palace, Abram notices how beautiful Sarai is and fears he will be killed because a more powerful male will be drawn to her beauty and slay him (Gen 12:11).

Sarai agrees to identify herself as Abram's sister, whereupon she is taken into the house of Pharaoh (Gen 12:15). King YHWH is livid when he learns that Abram's wife is living with Pharaoh and punishes him with plagues. Pharaoh, angry that he is punished for Abram and Sarai's lie, kicks them and everyone with them out of Egypt (Gen 12:20).

Abram and his clan return to *Beth El* near the altar he built to honor King YHWH. But disagreements between Abram and his nephew Lot force them to go their separate ways (Gen 13:11).

King YHWH returns to reassure Abram that he will receive great blessings (Gen 13:14-18). But again, rather than blessings, chaos ensues and a great war breaks out among the clans. Abram flees again, eventually arriving at Salem (trans. "peace"), the city ruled by *Melchi zadok*.[45]

Melchizedek brings out LHM and wine because he was the "Priest of LHM LLYN"; he says, "Blessed be Abram of *LHM LLYN*." Rendered *eLa Ha eM, eLa, eLyowN*, the words are translated, "Goddess the Mother Goddess Most High..."[46] (Gen 14:19).

This reveals that Abram's biological parents were not descended from King YHWH; Abram's parents were descended from King Eloah and Goddess the Mother. Perhaps Abram, like Moses after him, was secretly placed with a Judean woman who could protect him from a violent oppressor by claiming he was a Judean loyal to YHWH.

King YHWH returns to remind Abram, "To your descendants I give this land, from the river of Egypt to the great river, the river Euphrates, the land of the Kenites...Hittites...Canaanites..." et. al. (Gen 15:18-20).

"Sarai said to Abram, '...YHWH has prevented me from bearing children; go in to my maid; it may be that I shall obtain children by her" (Gen 16:2).

So, Hagar the Egyptian maid bore Abram a son, Ishmael.

Abram becomes *Abraham* at Gen 17:1-8: "When Abram was ninety-nine years old YHWH did *NOT* appear to Abram."

The Hebrew consonant *L* can be rendered *eL*[47] (trans. "to" and "God"), *Lo*[48] (trans. "not"), and *aL*[49] (also trans. "not"). The context determines the choice, and King YHWH had *not* visited Abram since before Ishmael was born when Abram was eighty-six years old (Gen 16:16).

In the intervening years, a "messenger of YHWH" aided with the conception and birth of Ishmael to Hagar, but King YHWH never returned.

So, after thirteen years with no communication from King YHWH, when Abram was nine-nine, he is approached by *Ela Shadday*, "Goddess with breasts."[50]

She says to him, "'I will make my covenant between me and you, and will make you exceedingly numerous.' Then Abram fell on his face; Goddess the Mother said, 'As for me, this is my covenant with you: You shall be the ancestor of a multitude of nations. No longer shall your name be Abram, but your name shall be Abraham; for I have made you the ancestor of a multitude of nations...I will make nations of you, and *kings shall come from you*...And I will give to you, and to your offspring after you, the land where you are now an alien, all the land of Canaan for a perpetual holding; and

I will be their LHM LLHM'" (Gen 17:1-8; emphasis added).

Ela Shadday has the power to produce kings, YHWH does not.

Ela Shadday tells Ab-raham that SHE will also be known to him and his offspring as *LHM* (trans. "Ela the Mother") LLHM, rendered *HaLaL Ha eM*[51] (trans. "Praise the Mother").

This is the feature of "Hellenistic Judaism" that has been hidden for two-thousand years: *El and Ela the Mother* are the ancestors of Abraham, Isaac, and Jacob.

The name *BRHM* gives Abraham several attributes. Rendered *BaR Ha Em*, he is identified as, "Son of the Mother." When rendered *aB RaHaM*,[52] he is "Father of Compassion." Rendered *aB ReHeM*,[53] he is "Father of Womb." Abram no longer exists to exult King YHWH; as Abraham he now serves his true family, King Eloah and Ela ha Em.

Eventually, the "deity" with Breasts addresses the problem of Sarai's barrenness:

"Ela the Mother said to Abraham, 'As for Sarai your wife, you shall not call her *Sarai*[54] but *Sarah*[55] shall be her name.[56] I will bless her, and moreover, I will give you a son by her. I will bless her, and she shall give rise to nations; *kings* of peoples shall come from her" (Gen 17:15-16).

SRH is *iSha RaH* and/or *aSha RaH,* the reviled goddess *Asherah* whose name is perhaps a combination of "man/woman" and "Rah," the Egyptian sun god.

"Then *LHM* said, '*BL* (*aB eL,* trans. "Father El") and your wife Sarah will bear you a son, and you will call him Isaac'" (Gen 17:19).

The name "Isaac" is from *tsachar,* defined as "reddish-gray; tawny" but translated "white" in the only example in the OT.[57] His father is King Eloah.

Sarai blamed King YHWH for her barrenness (Gen 16:2); Sarai remained barren until Ela Shadday renamed her *SaRaH* and/or *aShaRaH* and King Eloah impregnated her.

The kings and queens descended from Abraham and Sarah are known as *Ba'aL* (*aB'eL,* trans. "Father El") and *Asherah* (*Isha oR/Rah,* trans. "Woman Light/Sun").

26

Unfortunately for Baal and Asherah, King YHWH's descendants had a brilliant marketing strategy—demonize anyone who opposed him, especially those who, like Abraham and Sarah, supported and promoted the benevolent "Father-Mother."

Demonizing Baal[58] was executed with passion as YHWH's priests set about to acquire more followers and power. Fear of a vicious demon proved to be most effective for conversions and retention.

Merging Baal with Bezzle-bub, Lucifer, and Satan was the innovation that produced lasting effects that continue today among those who are susceptible to superstition. These superstitions are passed on to children, and books that offer alternative explanations based on reason are banned. The visceral terror of demonic forces supersedes logic, and the cycle continues generation to generation.

CHAPTER THREE

RACHEL AND JACOB

Goddess with breasts isn't heard from again until Sarah's son with King El is about to die. Isaac's wife Rebekah is concerned that her favorite son Jacob might be killed by his envious elder brother. Rebekah had encouraged Jacob to deceive Isaac in order to get the death-bed blessing meant for his elder son.

Rebekah instructs Jacob, "Now then, my son, do what I say: Flee at once to my brother Laban in Harran. Stay with him for a while until your brother's fury subsides. When your brother is no longer angry with you and forgets what you did to him, I'll send word for you to come back from there. Why should I lose both of you in one day?" (Gen 27:43-5).

Rebekah tells her dying husband Isaac, "I am weary of my life because of the Hittite women. If Jacob marries one of the Hittite women such as these...what good will my life be to me?" (Gen 27:45-6).

Isaac then blesses Jacob again, "May Ela Shadday bless you and make you fruitful and increase your numbers until you become a community of peoples... (and) pass on to you and your descendants the blessings promised to Abraham. May you own this land where you are now living as a foreigner, for LHM gave this land to Abraham" (Gen 28:3-4).

So Jacob sets out to find his mother's brother Laban, but he encounters Laban's daughter Rachel at a well where she has come to water her father's sheep. Jacob rolls away a heavy stone covering the well; soon he and Rachel fall in love. When Jacob asks his uncle for Rachel's hand, Laban attaches strings: Jacob must work for Laban seven years.

"So Jacob served seven years to get Rachel, but they seemed like only a few days to him because of his love for her" (Gen 29:20).

But Laban double-crosses Jacob; in the dark of night, he delivers his eldest daughter Leah instead, and Jacob makes love to her, believing her to be Rachel.

Needless to say, Jacob is a tad pissed. "When morning came, there was Leah! So Jacob said to Laban, 'What is this you have done to me? I served you for Rachel, didn't I? Why have you deceived me?' Laban replies, 'It is not our custom here to give the younger daughter in marriage before the older one.'" (Gen 29:25-6).

In exchange for an additional seven years of work, Jacob and Rachel finally become husband and wife.

However, as with all the daughters of Ela the Mother, Rachel and Leah are not impregnated by Jacob. The House of Jacob's first four sons were conceived when, "[King] YHWH saw that Leah was unloved, he opened her womb ... Leah conceived and bore a son ... Reuben ... She conceived again and bore a son ... Simeon ... she conceived and bore a son ... Levi ... She conceived again and bore a son ... Judah" (excerpts from Gen 29:31-35).

None of the first four sons was "conceived with" or "bore to Jacob." They were "conceived" when King YHWH opened Leah's womb.

Jacob's first two biological sons were born when Rachel offered him the handmaid Laban had given to her: "Jacob went into her and Bilhah conceived and *bore Jacob* a son" (Gen 30:4); "Rachel's maid Bilhah conceived again and *bore Jacob* a second son" (Gen 30:7). Bilhah's sons were Dan and Naphtali.

In addition, Zilpah, the handmaid Laban gave to Rachel's sister Leah, also "bore Jacob" two sons (Gen 30:10-12). Zilpah's sons were Gad and Asher.

At this point in the narrative, after four step-sons and four biological sons, the story seems to get weird:

"In the days of wheat harvest Reuben [Leah's eldest son] went and found mandrakes in the field, and brought them to his mother Leah. Then Rachel said to Leah, "Please give me some of your son's mandrakes. But she said to her, 'Is it a small matter that you have taken away my husband? Would you take away my son's mandrakes also?' Rachel said, 'Then he may lie with you tonight for your son's mandrakes. When Jacob came from the field in the evening, Leah went out to meet him, and said, 'You must *not*[59] come in to me; for I have traded[60] you with my son's mandrakes.' So he lay with her that night" (Gen 30:14-16).

Five references to "mandrakes" in these two verses certainly attracts attention. "Mandrakes," Hebrew, *duday*,[61] is from *dod*, defined as "beloved, love, uncle." The name "David" is from the same as *dod*.[62] "Mandrake" is used in these verses to identify a "beloved uncle" who impregnates Leah.

Reuben's uncles were his father's and mother's brothers; his mother's brothers are never named. Therefore, "uncle" must refer to his father's brother. King YHWH opened Leah's womb when she conceived Rueben and his three younger brothers. But who is King YHWH's brother?

In the *Enuma Elis*, which shares elements with the OT, Prince Ea's brother is Prince EnLiL; King YHWH is often attached to King Eloah as, "YHWH-LH," suggesting that YaH and Eloah may have been brothers or half-brothers. And indeed, Eloah appears in the scene just before Leah conceives thanks to "her son's uncle":

"And LHM and Eloah heard Leah, and she conceived and gave Jacob a fifth son. Leah said, 'LHM has lifted my status because I gave my maid to my

33

husband'; so she named him Issachar[63] (Gen 30:17-18).

"Leah conceived again and bore a sixth son to Jacob. Then Leah said, 'LHM has endowed me with a good gift; now my husband will dwell with me, because I have borne him six sons.' So she named him Zebulun" (Gen 30:19-20).

"Then LHM remembered Rachel and LHM listened, eLoah opened her womb, she conceived and bore a son...she named him 'Joseph'" (Gen 30:22-4).

Joseph is the House of Jacob's eleventh son, but Jacob isn't present when Joseph is conceived; his conception is attended by eLa Ha eM and Eloah, "the God" who "opened her womb." Joseph's biological father is King Eloah.

Jacob eventually returns to Bethel where Ela Shadday greets him. "Your name is Jacob, but you will no longer be called Jacob; your name will be Israel...I am Ela Shadday; be fruitful and increase in number. A nation and a community of nations will come from you, and **kings** will be among your descendants" (Gen 35:10-11).

The identity of the father of Rachel's second son is also shrouded in enigmas. Rachel named her son "Benoni," which means "son of my sorrow." However, "...his father called him Benjamin," which means "son of the right hand" (Gen 35:18).

The identity of "his father" is hidden in the Hebrew word for "right hand," *yamin*.[64] "Your right hand, O YHWH glorious in power – your right hand, O YHWH shattered the enemy" (Ex 15:6).

Rachel's second son was King YHWH's *ben yamin*. And once this *Virgin-Daughter of Goddess the Mother* produced a son with King Eloah and a son with King YHWH, her duty as the highest-ranking Temple Virgin was complete. Rachel was needed elsewhere to assume the duties of a *Goddess—Ela ha Em*: "So Rachel died, and she was buried on *the way* to *Ephrathah* (that is, *Bethlehem*)..."

The word *Ephrathah* is related to *ePheR*[65] (trans. "ashes"), a description of what is left after the Israelites' Asherah Poles are burned and her temples destroyed. It reveals important clues to the YHWH vs LHM battle for power.

"...the Israelites had sinned against YHWH; Eloah and Goddess the Mother had brought them up out of Egypt from under the power of Pharaoh king of

Egypt. They worshiped El and Ela ha Em and followed the practices of the nations that YHWH had driven out before them, as well as the practices that the kings of Israel had introduced. The Israelites secretly did things against YHWH...From watchtower[66] to fortified city they built themselves high places in all their towns. They set up sacred stones and Asherah poles on every high hill and under every flourishing tree" (2 Kings 17:7-10).

"So YHWH was very angry with Israel and removed them from his presence. Only the tribe of Judah was left, *and even Judah did not keep the commands of YHWH*. They followed the practices Israel had introduced" (2 Kings 17:18-19).

It seems that even Judeans preferred the benevolent Father-Mother over the merciless King YHWH. So, Kings known as *YHWH* set about to demonize and destroy Father-Mother—BaaL and Asherah—who are hated to this day.

This war between YHWH and LHM is a recurring theme throughout the Hebrew Bible. The balance of power shifts back and forth like the pendulum of political parties. Just as it seems that Father-Mother compassion is about to enter the hearts and minds of the masses, the violent tyrant rises again to threaten and kill the people of peace, Children of Eloah and Ela ha Em, "Children of Light":

> "'Believe in the light while you have the light, so that you may become children of light.' When he had finished speaking, Jesus left and hid himself from them" (John 12:36).

The word "Bethlehem" first appears at Gen 35:19-21:

"So Rachel died, and she was buried on *the way* to *ePaRaH*[67] (that is, *Bethlehem*), and Jacob set up a pillar at her grave; it is the pillar of Rachel's tomb, which is there to this day. Israel journeyed on, and pitched his tent beyond the *tower of Eder*"[68] Gen 35:21).

"*Jacob* set up a pillar," but "*Israel* journeyed on" after Rachel was buried on the way to BTLHM under the stone pillar called, *MaGDaLa eDeR* (trans. "Watchtower of the Flock.") This scene is the inspiration for Mark's "Mary Magdalene," and it refers to a prophesy fulfilled but ignored:

> "As for you, watchtower of the flock, stronghold of Daughter Zion, the former dominion will be restored

to you; queenship will come to Daughter Jerusalem." (Micah 4:8-10).

BTLHM (*Bet Lehem, Bet Elohim, Betulah Em* and *Bat El ha Em*) was not just a place; it was also the *identity and function* of royal women who traced their origins to Rachel.

Rachel's importance to Judaism and Christianity cannot be overstated, but her importance has been hidden by the men who created both. As a result, Rachel is identified, but not widely acknowledged, as *The Great Mother* in both traditions.

CHAPTER FOUR

RACHEL AND JOSEPH

At Gen 40, Rachel's son Joseph, now grown, has established a reputation for accurately interpreting dreams. Pharaoh's *Sar*[69] cupbearer and *Sar* baker[70] did something that angered him, so he put them in prison with Joseph.

They both had dreams and they asked Joseph to help find someone who could interpret them:

"And Joseph said to them, 'Do not interpretations belong to *LHM?* Please tell them to me'" (Gen 40:8).

So, the cupbearer told his dream to Joseph, and e*La ha eM's* interpretation predicts a happy ending (Gen 40:9-14).

The baker's dream is about three baskets on his head and birds eating from them. Expecting good news, the baker is disappointed. According to Joseph, LHM's interpretation was grim:

"The three baskets are three days; within three days Pharaoh will lift up your head—from you!—and crucify you on a pole; and the birds will eat the flesh from you...and it came to pass...*Sar aphah he crucified*, just as Joseph had interpreted to them" (Gen 40:18-22).

An important secret is hidden in Gen 40:22:

WTSRHPMTLHKSRPTRLHMYSP

Judean orthodox rendering:

We eT SaR Ha PaRaH TaLaH KaSaR PaTaR LaHeM YoSeP

Judean translation:

"...but the chief baker he crucified, just as predicted by Joseph."

Essene-Nazarene rendering:

We eT iSha oR, Ha PaRaH eT eLoaH Ki iSah oR PeTeR, eLa Ha eM YoSeP

Essene-Nazarene translation:

"But Woman Light is the Baker and Eloah's Woman of Light, the firstborn Goddess, the Mother of Joseph."

When Rachel was buried (Gen 35:19), enigmas hidden in words reveal what was to happen to her:

She was "...on the way to *Ephrathah* (that is BTLHM)."

From *Ephrathah* comes *apher,* translated "covering,"[71] and *aphah,*[72] translated "baker." *BeT eLa Ha eM* is the "House of Goddess the Mother," located in the *Temple of Rah* at Heliopolis in Egypt.

The enigmas say that after her "death," Rachel, the daughter of Goddess the Mother, would be found "under cover" disguised as "a baker" in Egypt where she would serve with her son in Pharaoh's court.

Joseph's Mother was *not* crucified (Genesis 40:23).[73]

WLZKRSRHMMSQMTYWSPWYYSKHH

We eLa ZaKaR, iSa RaHaM, MeSeQe,[74] eM eT
YoWSeP, WaY YiSKa HeHu

"But Goddess is male, a man with womb, heir,[75] Mother of Joseph, but forgotten."

Sarah and Ab-*racham*'s heir *Rachel*—Joseph's Mother disguised as a male—escaped crucifixion.

Two years after *The Baker* is unmasked as *Ela the Mother of Joseph,* Pharaoh has dreams that no one can interpret. The cupbearer tells him about Joseph's talent (Gen 41:14-15), so Pharaoh sends for Joseph.

"I have heard it said of you that when you hear a dream you can interpret it." Joseph's response is consistent: "It is not I; *LHM* will give Pharaoh a favorable answer."

Pharaoh describes his dreams and Joseph explains, "...*LHM* has revealed to Pharaoh what he is about to do" (Gen 41:25).

Ela ha Em interprets Pharaoh's dream as a premonition of seven years of rain and abundant crops followed by seven years of drought. LHM, through Joseph, advises Pharaoh to save one-fifth of each of the seven years of abundance for food during the drought.

As a reward, Pharaoh promotes Joseph to second in command over all of Egypt. Only Pharaoh has more power. And as an added bonus, he gives Joseph a wife, the daughter of the Priest of the Temple of the Sun.

This is the "Triumph of Joseph at the Court of the Pharoah," the story of a Nazar who became a slave, then a freedman and ruler, *whose Mother's wisdom was behind his success.*

CHAPTER FIVE

MARY THE MAGDALENE AND JESUS THE NAZARENE

Mark's play—*The Gospel According to Mark*—was a revised and updated version of the *Triumph of Joseph at the Court of the Pharaoh*. It was probably written during the reign of King Herod (c. 37 to c. 4 BCE) when Jewish leaders Nasi Hillel and Shammai (from *shama*, "hear/obey") led two competing schools of thought. Their descendants continued the two schools after their deaths until c. 37, concurrent with the reign of Emperor Caligula.

According to the *Jerusalem Talmud* (Shabbat 1:4 (3c)), the *House of Shammai* obtained their majority by killing members of the *House of Hillel*.

According to Yevamot 14b, each school kept track of its members' lineages and forbid marriage between the two schools,[76] a reminder of the forbidden relationships in Leviticus and a continuation of that tradition.

The *Talmud* notes, "with the advent of the *House of Hillel* and the *House of Shammai*, the Torah became like two Torahs."[77]

The traditions and translations carried forth from YHWH's Tribe of Judah were taught in the *House of Shammai* . The traditions and translations from LHM's Essene-Nazarenes were taught in the *House of Hillel*.

The *House of Hillel* continued through fourteen generations of leaders for nearly 400 years.[78] The *House of Shammai* was absorbed into Christianity after the Jewish Revolt, and it remained a competing sect for more than three centuries.

The grand finale in Mark's script was lost and has never been recovered. Perhaps it was abhorrent to

Paul and the priests. Their *God and Son of God* was invented to deny the Goddess and replace the scapegoat so corrupt, unethical people could continue self-serving schemes. Only fools would "treat others as they want to be treated" for Christ's sake!

Patriarchal priests and Paul refused to accept a *Son of God and Goddess* who volunteered to give His life that the Great Mother Goddess might be **saved.** Being a Goddess with Wisdom, Mother also **saved** her son.

Traditions suggest that the dramatic conclusion of Mark's Hebrew text was performed as the morning sun and Venus rose in the East. With a little imagination it can be reasonably recreated:

YHWH's priests condemn Goddess the Mother for the blasphemy of claiming to be a God. They ask Rome that she be crucified, just as Pharaoh crucified Joseph's mother "The Baker."

Joseph's son, *YaH-Zeus*, begs to take his Mother's place on the cross.

"Jesus cried out with a loud voice, [LLLMSBChTN] 'Eloi, Eloi, lema saba chthani,' (*which means My God, my God, why have you forsaken me?*)" (Mk 15:34).

The orthodox translation is a misdirection.

Hillel's Essene-Nazarene translation of LLLMSBChTN is *eLa, eLa, oLaM SaBa ChThaNi*, "Goddess, Goddess, eternal oath, Bridegroom." No longer is Jesus just "Son of God and Goddess"; now he is *Goddess the Mother's* son-in-law, the "bridegroom," as her daughter is crowned *The Goddess*.

Goddess the Mother and *The Bride* follow Yah-Zeus to the tomb, taking with them healing spices and herbs they have prepared to nourish him. After three days, Yah-Zeus emerges triumphant over death thanks to Mother and Bride's knowledge; knowledge that would later be associated with witchcraft and lead to executions of innocent women.

Mother greets him with a crown of laurel leaves which she places over the crown of thorns. Daughter places a modius pot on his head to identify him as Egypt's *Sarapis*[79] acknowledging Emperor Hadrian's lament, "The worshipers of Sarapis (here) are called Christians, and those who are devoted to the god Sarapis call themselves Bishops of Christ."[80]

"Jesus" wearing a crown of thorns and laurel leaves; and, The Egyptian god "Sar-apis" wearing a modius pot.
Painted panel, Roman Egypt, c. 100 CE

Then Mother places a wreath of laurel blossoms around her daughter's neck, making sure it covers her heart. The value of humility and compassion are recognized, giving equal reverence for women.

Hand-in-hand, the three lead the way to *BTLHM,* followed by a jubilant crowd, dancing and singing, "Halal Ela! Halal El!"[81]

At the *House of Goddess the Mother*, wreaths of laurel decorate a round table covered in the white linen from the empty tomb. Vestal Virgins serve *Mola Salsa Wafers* and sacred spring water. Curious observers are invited to join in, assorted breads and wine are added, and the celebration continues until a full week has passed.[82]

However, not everyone was joyful. YHWH"s priests were terrified that this Goddess—a former slave— might empower women and slaves, heaven forbid! Paul's Christianity caught fire with insecure men. Plus, vicarious atonement was far more appealing than sharing with those less fortunate.

Fear of women and freedmen[83] in positions of power, fueled by Paul's anti-women and pro-slavery propaganda, exploded into the *First Jewish Revolt* that lasted four years (66-70).

It began when the High Priest Matthias plagiarized and interpolated Mark's script. His *Gospel According to Matthew* successfully separated "Jesus the Nazarene" from "Joseph the Nazar" by claiming "The Nazarene" meant "Jesus came from Nazareth" (Mt 2:23).

This agenda-driven lie required interpolations to Mark's Hebrew-language script which read, "Jesus came from BTLHM..." (Mk 1:9). BTLHM was replaced with "Nazareth" to support Mt 2:23.

But removing BTLHM inadvertently removed "Virgin Mother" *(BeTuLaH eM)*, "Daughter of Goddess the Mother" *(BaT eLa Ha eM)*, and the "Little Town of *BeTLeHeM*." After Matthew interpolated Mark and published his own gospel of lies, Luc, a Nazarene (possibly Luc Plutarchus[84]) attempted to repair the damage. Later, another Nazarene (possibly Polycarp[85]) added *Acts of the Apostles* which reveals Paul's participation in the conspiracy to bury the Goddess.

This unknown author who claims to be Luc reviews the history of *Ela Shadday* from Abraham to *Joseph the Nazar* and his *Triumph at the Court of the Pharaoh.*[86]

Most biblical scholars, including three popular authors, Dennis McDonald, Bart Ehrman and Richard Carrier, support the consensus that Matthew and Luke relied on Mark to compose their texts.

McDonald and Ehrman also support the *Q Source* theory[87] to explain elements in Matthew and Luke that cannot be found in Mark.

Carrier rejects the existence of Q, noting a common-sense sequence puts both Mark and Matthew into Luke's hands. Therefore, he argues, Matthew added "Virgin Mother" and "Bethlehem" and Luke included these additions in his gospel.

A third option, with evidence, is a Hebrew Mark.

Unfortunately, nearly all scholars have stubbornly rejected Jean Carmignac's discovery, reported in his book, *The Birth of the Synoptic Gospels*[88] that proto-Mark was written in Hebrew and translated into Greek.[89]

BTLHM, both *Virgin Mother* and *Bethlehem*, was the feature of *The Gospel According to Mark* that Matthew had to remove to support his "Jesus from Nazareth" lie. The original word at Mk 1:9 was the Hebrew BTLHM.

The Great Revolt ended in 70 when Roman soldiers reclaimed the Temple destroying it in the process. The Romans were victorious, but *Paul's Heresy* was not eradicated. Shammai's priests were allowed to remain active in Jerusalem to moderate orthodox Jews.

The church fathers loyal to Paul were determined to hide Jesus the Nazarene's descent from Joseph the Nazar's Goddess Mother—The Baker. Priests and Bishops continued to stoke the embers of fear in the minds of insecure and superstitious men until an Emperor they could control rose to power.

Circa 306, Constantine became Emperor of Rome. Circa 380, all other faiths became heresies, especially *The Way of the Nazarene.* Anyone practicing a competing religion was tortured, converted, and/or killed. Faith in vicarious atonement triumphed over Jesus' teachings of unconditional love, peaceful coexistence, and compassion.

Now read Mark's gospel and replace the word "God" with LHM, "Goddess the Mother" or "God and Goddess." What a wondrous message for all the mothers and daughters of the world! And fathers and sons might want to take note as well.

Jesus' message—prior to Paul's humongous lie to honor YHWH and to spite that Empress bitch—was that women are equal—if not superior—to men.

Luc Plutarchus left a clue to help scholars understand how to read "stories about the gods":

> "Whenever you hear the traditional tales...about the gods, their wanderings, dismemberments, and many experiences [i.e., "deaths"]...you must not think that any of these tales actually happened in the manner in which they are related.
> "If you listen to the stories about the gods in this way...you may avoid superstition which is no less an evil than atheism."[90]

CHAPTER SIX

CLEOPATRA

AND

JULIUS CAESAR

On October 20, 415, Nicene-Christian Emperors Honorius and Theodosius II issued an edict that stripped the last Nasi of his rank of honorary prefect. Nasi Gamaliel VI was banned from adjudicating disputes between Jews and Christians, converting men and women to *The Way of the Nazarenes*,[91] and employing slaves, also known as "Freedmen."[92]

The *Codex Theodosianus*[93] refers to an edict in 426 that transformed the Nasi's tax into an imperial tax, suggesting the last Nasi, Gamaliel VI, died c. 425. This was the end of the *House of Hillel*; the *House of Shammai* (by now fully absorbed into Christianity) was left to flourish with Judaism as the only competition.

His assumed ancestor, Nasi Gamaliel[94] I (c. 15 BCE to c. 74 CE),[95] was the grandson of Nasi Hillel. Coincidentally, Hillel showed up in Jerusalem shortly after Julius Caesar was assassinated in Rome.

Emperor Honorius, working with Bishop Epiphanius, united Church and State and declared *Nicene Christianity* the only official and permitted religion of the Roman Empire.[96] Bands of Christian soldiers traveled throughout the Empire destroying temples and other structures dedicated to gods and goddesses. The Temple of Zeus, the Temple of Apollo, the Temple of Sarapis in Alexandria, and the Temple of the Vestal Virgins were all destroyed.

Honorius, Theodosius II, and Epiphanius attempted to destroy all of Hillel's teachings and all evidence of their existence. The best of times for women and slaves came to an abrupt end.

But enigmatic clues remained awaiting discovery:

The Baker's Tomb is a monument constructed next to the Porta Maggiore, Rome's East Gate, a virtual duplicate of Jerusalem's East Gate. The couple whose remains were interred there are identified as *former slaves* who became successful *bakers*, inspired by *Joseph the Nazar and his Mother,* but still unacknowledged by the men in power.

Circa 420, after Paul's Christianity became the official religion of Rome, Honorius ordered workers to bury the *Baker's Tomb* and the *Porta Maggiore* under a massive stone structure, also called "Porta Maggiore." Apparently, something in the Baker's Tomb threatened the Nicene- Christian agenda.

But what did Honorius see in Rome's East Gate and a "freed slave's monument to his trade" that led him to bury these structures during the same era other heretical temples were being destroyed? How might a *gate* and a *tomb* be connected to temples built to honor Greek and Roman Gods, Goddesses, and Vestal Virgins? The fact that they *were* buried demands answers to these questions.

The Baker's Tomb would have been a big part of the annual Crucifixion-Resurrection Festival that honored *The Baker and Her Son*. These celebrations would have carried into the time the destructions began in earnest and the Porta Maggiore and the Baker's Tomb were buried.

Perhaps more revealing is the decree by Pope Gregory XVI in 1838 that ordered the Baker's Tomb uncovered. This suggests that all the Emperors, Bishops and Popes up to his time must have known the identities of the couple in the buried *House of Bread*.

In 1839, the year after exposing the long-buried tomb of freedmen bakers, Pope Gregory XVI wrote an apostolic letter forbidding the Faithful to participate in the Atlantic Slave Trade. These brief excerpts are worth reading, especially in today's political climate:

> "...we have judged that it belonged to Our pastoral solicitude to exert Ourselves to turn away the Faithful from the inhuman slave trade in Negroes and all other men...desiring to remove such a shame from all the Christian nations...We warn and adjure earnestly in the Lord faithful Christians of every condition that no one in the future dare to...reduce

to servitude, or lend aid and favor to those who give themselves up to these practices, or exercise that inhuman traffic by which the Blacks, as if they were not men but rather animals, having been brought into servitude, in no matter what way, are, without any distinction, in contempt of the rights of justice and humanity..."

Twenty-two years later, following the election of Abraham Lincoln, Confederate forces determined to preserve slavery attacked Fort Sumter; America's Civil War had begun. How much blame—or credit—belongs to Pope Gregory is anyone's guess. But it seems certain that his efforts were important to the cause of freedom for all, regardless of class or color.

Unfortunately, freedom for all is yet to be realized.

Wikipedia sources date the tomb's construction to c. 50-20 BCE. However, evidence for a later date comes from *The Archaeology of Rome* by John Henry Parker (1806–1884). Parker was an English archaeologist who specialized in ancient architecture, and in 1877, he challenged the BCE dating.

Parker argues that the tomb was built after the aqueducts and after Claudius constructed Rome's East

Gate, the *Porta Maggiore*, which identifies Rome as "The New Jerusalem" (52 CE).[97]

Additional artifacts discovered near the tomb provide clues to the identities of the interred couple. Parker notes:

"The tomb was much mutilated, and the second inscription had to be collected from fragments, and amongst them was a sculpture in bas-relief of the baker Eurysacis[98] and his wife Atistia."[99]

Marble Relief of Eurysacis and Atistia[100]

Photograph by P.J. Gott, June, 2015

The name, *Eury sacis* is translated "wide small," an apt description of the gates of Claudius' Porta Maggiore pictured below with the Baker's Tomb.

Eury and *sacis* could have been chosen to refute any attempt to date the tomb prior to the Porta Maggiore's construction that features *wide* and *narrow* gates.

Clues to the identities of *Eurysacis* and *Atistia* can be teased from inscriptions written in Latin:

EST HOC MONIMENTVM
MARCEI VERGILEI EVRYSACIS
PISTORIS REDEMPTORIS APPARET

Note the oversized "T," one in each word, that resembles the *Roman Tau Crucifix*.[101] These words are generally translated, "baker, contractor, public servant." However, this translation is acknowledged to be problematic:

APPARET is erroneously translated as a noun ("public servant"); *apparet* is a verb that means "...to come in sight, to appear..."[102] Therefore, the intended translation is more likely, "appeared."

REDEMPTORIS is translated "contractor," but another valid word is "redeemed," as *Goddess the Mother* was redeemed.

PISTORIS, "Baker," refers to Joseph's Mother, the first crucifixion in the Bible and the Goddess who disguised herself as a male.

A better translation:

BAKER REDEEMED APPEARED

This might have been reason enough for Honorius to bury the Baker's Tomb, but the inscribed names also carry clues that expose the deception and restore the truth about Jesus and his Mother:

MARCEI refers to the god Mars, the father of twins Romulus and Remus, mythological founders of Rome; their mother, Rhea Silvia, was a Vestal Virgin.[103] Emperor Tiberius was the paternal grandfather of twin boys whose maternal grandmother was Antonia, Marc Antony's daughter.[104]

VERGILEI refers to Vestal Virgins, the preeminent bakers in the Roman Empire. Vestals led the annual New Year rites on March 1 when new laurel branches replaced the old branches as they relit the sacred fire to symbolize a fresh start of the New Year.[105] The epitaph found with the bas-relief portrait is written in Latin:

FVIT ATISTIA VXOR MIHEI

Atistia was my wife

FEMINA OPITVMA VEIXSIT

A most excellent lady in life

QVOIVS CORPORIS RELIQVIAE

the surviving remains of her body

QUOD SVPERANT SVNT IN

which are in

HOC PANARIO

this breadbasket[106]

Note again the oversized "T" in the words FVIT ("was") and the first "T" in *ATIS TIA*. Note also the slight space between *ATIS* and *TIA*, names of deities popular in the Roman Empire when the tomb was constructed.

The festival for Atis was the *Ides of March*, Rome's most important holiday. So important, in fact, that Julius Caesar died on March 15, 44 BCE, the *first* day of the *Ides of March*, and Emperor Tiberius died on March 16, 37 CE, the *second* day of the *Ides of March*. Quite a coincidence had they died "in the manner related."[107]

Emperor Claudius formalized the week-long festival as a Roman holiday c. 54, about the time the Porta Maggiore was constructed.

March 15 was celebrated as the day Atis was born and discovered among the reeds of a river (as was Moses).

A week later, March 22, priests cut down a tree, hung an image of Atis on it, and carried it to the temple of the Great Mother Goddess. This commemorated Atis' death under a pine tree after he castrated himself. Three days of mourning followed, and the festival concluded on March 25 when Atis was reborn.[108]

Atis was a god without a penis, helpful when a "goddess" needed to disguise herself as a male – as Joseph's mother did.[109]

Tia, in *Atis-tia*, may refer to *Theia* (also *Thia*; *Thea*), the Greek Goddess of Light. Her brother/consort is Hyperion, god of the sun. They are the parents of Helios ("Sun"), Selene ("Moon"), and Eos ("Dawn"). [110]

Queen Cleopatra named her twins *Alexander **Helios*** and *Cleopatra **Selene***. Selene's father was Marcus Antonius; she married King Juba II. Their daughter, Antony and Cleopatra's granddaughter, dropped out of sight, her name unknown. Curiously, she is memorialized in Athens as, "Juba's daughter" in two inscriptions discovered near the location of the statue of Pallas-Athena, moved from Athens c. 465 CE and later destroyed.[111]

To earn two inscriptions near the statue of Athena, this mysterious granddaughter of Antony and Cleopatra must have done something remarkable. Tradition suggests she was probably named after her mother and grandmother, Cleopatra **Thea Philo** Pater.

Juba II was married a second time to princess Glaphyra of Cappadocia, the widow of Alexander III, whose parents were Herod the Great, King of Judea, and Hasmonean Jewish princess, Mariamme.

Alexander IV (Herod and Mariamme's grandson) disappeared from history as mysteriously as had Antony and Cleopatra's granddaughter.[112]

Curiously, Alexander IV's contemporary, also called "Alexander," arrived in Alexandria with two sons and a *brother*, but with no wife or any information about their family or ancestors.

Alexander[113] "the Alabarch" managed extensive lands in Egypt owned by Antonia Minor. Antonia's sons (Antony's grandsons) were Claudius and Germanicus.[114]

Alexander's Jewish title, *Alabarch* (LBRK), can also be rendered *eLa BaRaK*, translated "Goddess blessed."

Like Juba and Selene's daughter, Alexander's wife is a mystery.

The first century poet Ovid associates Selene with the goddess Pallas;[115] Claudius' freedman *Marcus Antonius Pallas*[116] was so wealthy and so powerful that Pliny the Younger[117] wrote about him in two letters addressed to his friend Montanus.

The first describes the location of a monument built to honor Pallas "on the road to Tiber," a road that passed through Claudius' Porta Maggiore and right by the Baker's Tomb. The second letter is quite lengthy and filled with over-the-top complaints about the honors bestowed on a lowly freedman.[118]

Perhaps the letters were written to preserve a record of the honors awarded to Pallas.[119] But why would they need to be preserved in a letter that complains about them?

What did Selene's daughter do to be memorialized in Athens? And, why don't we know her name? Was she, perhaps, known by more than one name?

Was Alabarch Alexander's *brother* Philo his step-*sister*, a woman philosopher disguised as a man?

Was "Alabarch Alexander" also known as, *Alexander IV*, whose unnamed step-sister was Philo, the missing but inscription-worthy daughter of Juba and Selene?

Did Anthony and Cleopatra's unnamed grand-daughter marry her step-brother, the missing grandson of King Herod and Jewish princess Mariamme?

The last "Saying" in The Gospel of Thomas has sparked debate among scholars since it was discovered at Nag Hammadi in 1945 and published in a modern language in 1959. It's a thread that ties in here:

"Simon Peter said... 'Let's put Mary out of our group, for women are not worthy of life.'"

"Jesus replied, '...I myself will lead her to make her male, so that even she may become a live spirit, like you males; for every female making herself male will come under the imperial rule of heaven.'" (Gospel of Thomas, Saying 114).[120]

Jesus seems to suggest that if Mary were disguised as a male, her accomplishments would be considered valuable and therefore memorialized.

If Jesus helped Mary disguise herself as a male, who was the "he" that was Mary Magdalene?

Pallas the Freedman and *Philo of Alexandria* were contemporaries. Another coincidence?

Was *Atis Tia* also known as "Pallas the freedman"? Was she *Philo of Alexandria*? Was she *Mary the*

Magdalene? Was she all three, hence memorialized as "Juba's daughter"?

The question that immediately comes to mind is, wouldn't her voice give her away? Pliny the Younger's friend, Tacitus, answers that anticipated question:

> "...the proved innocence of Pallas did not please men so much as his arrogance offended them. When his freedmen, his alleged accomplices, were called, they reported that at home Pallas signified his wishes only by a nod or a gesture, or, if further explanation was required, *he used writing, so as not to degrade his voice* in such company."[121]

"Atis Tia" solves the mystery of Juba's daughter. The name "Atis" suggests the entombed woman had been disguised as a male deity, a god without a penis, yet another connection to *The Triumph of Joseph at the Court of the Pharaoh*.

"Yah-Zeus the Nazarene" is a god invented to peacefully absorb Judaism's YHWH into LHM's *The Way of the Nazarene*. An annual celebration of *Joseph's Triumph*, the triumph of *Goddess the Mother*, competed with Passover to entertain and convert YHWH's faithful.

But demons, eternal fires of hell, and burning at the stake[122] gave the *House of Shammai* the victory over Father-Mother of Compassion.

Unfortunately, the final victory of science over superstition cannot be celebrated until respected scholars examine the evidence, test Philo's Method, then convince skeptics of its validity. We do not have the scholarly qualifications required to break this fever of superstition. We are only qualified to solve puzzles.

Thank Goddess the geniuses who created "Jesus the Nazarene" left the proof of who they were in more than one artifact.

More precise and more informative than the Baker's Tomb is the Cameo that has been dated to the first century. It is currently housed at the *Bibliothèque Nationale* in Paris.

The Cameo was included among thirty or so items listed on the invoice as ***"relics of Christ"*** that reached Paris in 1239. Other "relics of Christ" in the shipment were "The Crown of Thorns" and "The Image of Edessa."

Circa 1620, when the Julio-Claudian Dynasty was recognized as the men and women depicted, the Cameo was quietly renamed "The Great Cameo of France."

Opinions differ regarding the characters; however, most are identified by the objects depicted with them.

Floating in Heaven, the deceased (left to right):

Marcus Antonius ("Mark") holding the Roman Generals' Shield of Zeus and Athena;

Emperor Augustus Julius Caesar (aka, *Octavian*) holding the ruler's Scepter of Zeus and Athena;

Queen Cleopatra, holding the Egyptians' *Eye of Rah*, representing the Spirit of Isis; Asherah; Ela the Mother;

Gaius Julius Caesar on Pegasus, the mythological Steed of Zeus and Pallas-Athena, representing the Spirit of Zeus; YaH-Zeus; Abba-Eloah the Father.

The small figure between Cleopatra and Julius Caesar is the *Lares of Augustus*, "identified with the inaugural day of Imperial Roman magistracies and with Augustus himself."[123]

The middle row depicts the next three generations (left to right):

Julia Minor, Augustus' granddaughter. Emperor-to-be Nero sits on her lap. Born c. 37, little Nero dates this inauguration-celebration to c. 41;

Germanicus, Marc Antony's grandson, Antonia Minor's son; Emperor Tiberius' adopted son. When Germanicus "died," Alabarch Alexander was "born";

Agrippina Major, Augustus' granddaughter, wife of Germanicus;

Emperor Tiberius, passing the Shield of Zeus and Athena to Germanicus and Agrippina, the couple most likely to have portrayed *YH-Zeus* and *The Magdalene* in annual festivals, thus qualifying the Cameo as a *Relic of Christ*. Circumstantial evidence suggests that Germanicus/Alexander was also known as "Nasi Gamaliel I," a name that identifies him as the earthly representation of Goddess and God; his grandfather was Nasi Hillel the Elder.

Tiberius allegedly died on March 16, 37, the Ides of March, as did Julius Caesar in 44 BCE. Tiberius' image on the cameo suggests their "deaths" during that important holiday was merely a passing of the Scepter and Shield of Zeus and Pallas Athena to the next generation of Nazars.

The woman sitting on the throne next to Tiberius is the *Great Mother* of the woman known as *Philo, Pallas, Attis, Agrippina,* and *Mary Magdalene.* She is,

Cleopatra Selene, Cleopatra's daughter.

Emperor Claudius appears to be reaching for the Scepter of Zeus and Pallas-Athena which Tiberius holds out of his reach while facing Germanicus and Agrippina. This suggests the transition of power from Gaius (Caligula) to Claudius in 41 did not happen as reported.[124]

Agrippina Minor, wife of Claudius; daughter of Germanicus and Agrippina;

Marcus Amelius Lepidus is easily overlooked, seated on the floor beneath the Queen's throne. His biography begins with, "some areas of his lineage are unclear."[125]

Similarly, portions of Emperor Caligula's life are missing, suggesting possible altering of historians' texts to hide a humongous secret. And, the lineage of another historical man is also quite sparse:

Marcus Aemilius Lepidus was the son of Lucius Aemilius *Paulus* and the grandson of *Paulus* Aemilius Lepidus. Julia Minor was his mother; Germanicus and Agrippina were his uncle and aunt; Augustus was his maternal grandfather; Marcus Antonius was his great-grandfather. Why "Paulus" isn't a part of his name is a humongous mystery.

The Queen Mother's middle finger suggests her animosity toward this Julio-Claudian mystery man, depicted as crushed and dejected. Shortly before the Inauguration Cameo was commissioned c.41-2 the emperor called "Caligula" was *assassinated*[126] after he imprisoned and threatened to kill Philo's brother, Alabarch Alexander.[127] The Empress' finger may have provoked this cloaked Paulus to rebel against her and her daughters and sons, leading to the Great Jewish Revolt and Rome's destruction of YHWH's temple. And yes, the middle finger was a thing at the time.[128]

The lower level may depict sons and daughters of the figures in the middle row, future actors and actresses who would portray mythological characters in annual festivals in Rome, Alexandria, Jerusalem, and elsewhere: *Attis and Cybele*; *Sarapis and Isis*; *YH-Zeus and The Magdalene*.

The actors were historical men and women, all Julio-Claudians, a Dynasty birthed by the biological parents of Caesarion, also known as Ptolemy XV, better known as Emperor Tiberius.

Suetonius, Tacitus, the Plinys, Josephus, Ovid, and other historians were members of this family whose works were critical to preserving the history which Paul's Church worked so hard to destroy.

The lives of the Julio-Claudian Dynasty are scattered among a multitude of names and places in enigma-filled histories (i.e., Plutarch, Nicholas of Damascus, Suetonius, Tacitus, and Josephus).

The best known are the two Patriarchs and the Matriarch, a trio whose lives after their deaths are also hidden behind many names:

Cleopatra, Julius Caesar and Mark Antony

APPENDIX

Philo's Rules for identifying and solving enigmas, clues that say, "look for an alternative version."

1. The doubling of a phrase.
2. An apparently superfluous expression in the text.
3. The repetition of statements previously made.
4. A change of phraseology – all these phenomena point to something special that the reader must consider.
5. An entirely different meaning may also be found by disregarding the ordinarily accepted division of the sentence into phrases and clauses and by considering a different combination of the words.
6. Synonyms [and phonetically similar words] must be carefully studied.
7. A play upon words must be utilized for finding a deeper meaning.

8. A definite, allegorical [enigmatical] sense may be gathered from certain particles, adverbs, prepositions, [unclear pronoun antecedents], etc., and in certain cases it can be gathered even from

9. the part of a word.

10. Every word must be explained in *all its meanings* in order that different interpretations may be found.

11. The skillful interpreter may make slight changes in a word, following the rabbinical rule: "Read not so, but so." Philo, therefore, changed accents, breathings, etc., in Hebrew words.

12. Any peculiarity in a phrase justifies the assumption that some special meaning is intended. Details regarding the form of words are very important.

13. Consider the number of the word, if it shows any peculiarity in the singular or the plural: the tense of the verb, etc.

14. The gender of the noun may carry a clue.

15. Note the presence or omission of the article;

16. the artificial interpretation of a single expression;

17. the position of the verses of a passage;

18. peculiar verse combinations;
19. noteworthy omissions;
20. striking statements [i.e., angel, spirit, Holy Spirit, omen, prophecy, etc.];
21. numeral symbolism [i.e., Platonic; Gematria].

BOOKS BY GOTT AND LICHT USED AS SOURCE MATERIAL

Following Philo In Search of The Magdalene, the Virgins, the Men Called Jesus:
https://www.amazon.com/Following-Philo-Magdalene-Virgin-Called/dp/1934223069

Following Philo From Baal and Asherah to Jesus and Mary Magdalene:
https://www.amazon.com/Following-Philo-Asherah-Jesus-Magdalene/dp/1934223077

Jesus the Nazarene Son of God and Goddess

https://www.amazon.com/Jesus-Nazarene-Son-God-Goddess-ebook/dp/B09CG7FMCQ

ENDNOTES

[1] Cameo images photographed by: Marie-Lan Nguyen (User:Jastrow), 2008. The gesture goes back to Greco-Roman time.

[2] Iamblichus' Life of Pythagoras: www.gutenberg.org/files/63300/63300-h/63300-h.htm

[3] "Return to Zion," Wikipedia: https://en.wikipedia.org/wiki/Return_to_Zion

[4] "Biblical Hebrew from after the Babylonian exile in 587 BCE is known as 'Late Biblical Hebrew'. Late Biblical Hebrew shows Aramaic influence in phonology, morphology, and lexicon, and this trend is also evident in the later-developed Tiberian vocalization system." See "Biblical Hebrew: Eras," paragraph 4. Wikipedia: https://en.wikipedia.org/wiki/Biblical_Hebrew

[5] Plutarch, c. 46—c. 120 CE.

[6] Excerpt from Plutarch's *Moralia*, "Isis and Osiris."

[7] Philo of Alexandria, c. 10 BCE—c. 74CE.

[8] Clement of Alexandria, c. 150 CE to unknown.

[9] (Kirby 2001-2015) Clement of Alexandria, Stromata, Peter Kirby, 2001-2015, Early Christian Writings (I.15).

[10] "Nebuchadnezzar II," Wikipedia: www.en.wikipedia.org/wiki/Nebuchadnezzar_II

[11] *Nazar:* Strong's Hebrew 5144,

Biblehub: https://biblehub.com/hebrew/5144.htm: "to   dedicate, consecrate"

Nezer: Strong's Hebrew 5145,

Biblehub: https://biblehub.com/ hebrew/5145.htm: "consecration, crown, Naziriteship"

Nazir: Strong's Hebrew 5139,

Biblehub: https://biblehub.com /hebrew/5139.htm: "one consecrated, devoted"

[12] "Hellenistic Judaism,"

Wikipedia: https://en.wikipedia.org/ wiki/Hellenistic_Judaism

[13] "Septuagint,"

Wikipedia: https://en.wikipedia.org/ wiki/Septuagint

[14] "Hellenist" is from Hebrew words, *halel El*, trans. "Praise Eloah." Strong's Hebrew 1984b,

Biblehub: https://biblehub.com/ hebrew/1984b.htm

[15] "Salome Alexandra":

Wikipedia: https://en.wikipedia.org/wiki/Salome_Alexandra

[16] "Septuagint":

Wikipedia: https://en.wikipedia.org/ wiki/Septuagint

[17] Ibid

[18] *Asherah:* Strong's Hebrew 842,

Biblehub: https://biblehub.com/hebrew/842.htm

"Asherah," World History: https://www.worldhistory.org/ Asherah/

[19] *Ashtarot:* Strong's Hebrew 6252,

Biblehub: https://biblehub.com hebrew/haashtarot_6252.htm

[20] *bara*: Strong's Hebrew 1254,

Biblehub: https://biblehub.com/hebrew/1254.htm

[21] *zakar*: Strong's Hebrew 2134,

Biblehub: https://biblehub.com/hebrew/2145.htm

[22] *neqab*: Strong's Hebrew 5347,

Biblehub: https://biblehub.com/hebrew/5347.htm

[23] "Enuma Elish": Wikipedia: https://en.wikipedia.org/ wiki/EnumaElis

[24] In Aeneid, written between 29 and 19 BCE, Vergil, honors the deified Julius Caesar with this catchy little phrase: "Go forth with new value, boy: thus is the path to the stars; A son of gods that will have gods as sons." (Virg-el suggests a "Virgin of El" as the author.)

[25] *yatsar*: Strong's Hebrew 3334,

Biblehub: https://biblehub.com/hebrew/3334.htm

[26] *tsarar*: Strong's Hebrew 6887,

Biblehub: https://biblehub.com/hebrew/6887.htm

[27] *peri*: Strong's Hebrew 6529,

Biblehub: https://biblehub.com/hebrew/6529.htm

[28] *pera*: Strong's Hebrew 6545,

Biblehub: https://biblehub.com/hebrew/6545.htm

[29] *adamah*: Strong's Hebrew 127,

Biblehub: https://biblehub.com/hebrew/127.htm

[30] See "Europe's oldest known humans mated with Neandertals surprisingly often": www.sciencenews.org/article/europe-oldest-known-humans-mated-neandertals-dna-fossils

[31] *chavvah*: Strong's Hebrew 2332,

Biblehub: https://biblehub.com/hebrew/2332.htm

[32] *ishshah*: Strong's Hebrew 802,

Biblehub: https://biblehub.com/hebrew/802.htm

[33] *ish*: Strong's Hebrew 376,

Biblehub: https://biblehub.com/hebrew/376.htm

[34] *yada*: Strong's Hebrew 3045,

Biblehub: https://biblehub.com/hebrew/3045.htm

[35] *yadah*: Strong's Hebrew 3034,

Biblehub; https://biblehub.com/hebrew/3034.htm

[36] *qaniti*: Strong's Hebrew 7069,

Biblehub; https://biblehub.com/hebrew/7069.htm

[37] *ish*: Strong's Hebrew 376,

Biblehub; https://biblehub.com/hebrew/376.htm

[38] *tson*: Strong's Hebrew 6629,

Biblehub: https://biblehub.com/hebrew/6629.htm

[39] *esh*: Strong's Hebrew 784,

Biblehub: https://biblehub.com/hebrew/784.htm

[40] *nephesh*: Strong's Hebrew 5315,

Biblehub: https://biblehub.com/hebrew/5315.htm

[41] *nazar*: Strong's Hebrew, 5144,

Biblehub: https://biblehub.com/hebrew/5144.htm; .

[42] *nezer*: Strong's Hebrew 5145,

Biblehub: https://biblehub.com/hebrew/5145.htm;

[43] *sar*: Strong's Hebrew 8269, Biblehub,
https://biblehub.com/hebrew/8269.htm: chief, ruler, prince.

[44] *abram*: Strong's Hebrew 87, Biblehub,
https://biblehub.com/hebrew/87.htm

[45] *melek*: Strong's Hebrew 4428, "King"

Biblehub: https://biblehub.com/hebrew/4428.htm; *zadok* (tsedeq: Strongs Hebrew 6664, "righteousness."

Biblehub: https://biblehub.com/hebrew/6664.htm

[46] *elyown*: Strong's Hebrew 5945,

Biblehub: https://biblehub.com/hebrew/5945.htm

[47] *eL*: Strong's He1brew 413,

Biblehub: https://biblehub.com/hebrew/413.htm

[48] *Lo*: Strong's Hebrew 3808,

Biblehub: https://biblehub.com/hebrew/3808.htm

[49] *aL*: Strong's Hebrew 409,

Biblehub: https://biblehub.com/hebrew/409.htm

[50] *shad*: Strong's Hebrew 7699, Biblehub, "breast."

Biblehub: https://biblehub.com/hebrew/7699.htm.

Gen 49:25: "...your father's God...blessings of the breast and womb."

[51] *halal*: Strong's Hebrew 1984, Biblehub,
https://biblehub.com/hebrew/1984b.htm

[52] *raham*: Strong's Hebrew 7356, Biblehub,
https://biblehub.com/hebrew/7356.htm

[53] *rehem*: Strong's Hebrew 7358, Biblehub,
https://biblehub.com/hebrew/7358.htm

[54] *sar*: Strong's Hebrew 8269, Biblehub,
https://biblehub.com/hebrew/8269.htm

[55] *raah*: Strong's Hebrew 7200, Biblehub,
https://biblehub.com/hebrew/7200.htm: to see; appear

[56] *iShah oR RaaH* (SaRaH) is the name of the royal virgin of light who appeared among the people. Her descendants are identified by the prefix Sar.

[57] *tsachar*, Strong's Hebrew 6713,

Biblehub: https://biblehub.com/hebrew/6713.htm

[58] "Bael (demon)":

Wikipedia: https://en.wikipedia.org/wiki/Bael_(demon)

[59] *aL*: Strong's Hebrew 409,

Biblehub: https://biblehub.com/hebrew/409.htm

[60] *karah*: Strong's Hebrew 3739,

Biblehub: https://biblehub.com/hebrew/3739.htm

[61] *duday*: Strong's Hebrew 1736,

Biblehub: https://biblehub.com/hebrew/1736.htm

[62] *dod*: Strong's Hebrew 1730,

Biblehub: https://biblehub.com/hebrew/1730.htm

[63] *Yissaskar*: Strong's Hebrew 3485, Biblehub, https://biblehub.com/hebrew/3485.htm, from *nasa*: Strong's Hebrew 5375, Biblehub, https://biblehub.com/hebrew/5375.htm and

sakar: Strong's Hebrew 7939, Biblehub, https://biblehub.com/hebrew/7939.htm

[64] *yamin*: Strong's Hebrew 3225,

Biblehub: https://biblehub.com/hebrew/3225.htm

[65] *epher*: Strong's Hebrew 665, Biblehub, https://biblehub.com/hebrew/665.htm

[66] *migdol/magdal*, Strong's Hebrew 4026,

Biblehub: https://biblehub.com/hebrew/4026.htm

[67] *parah from Ephrathah*: Strong's Hebrew 6509, Biblehub, https://biblehub.com/hebrew/6509.htm defined as: to bear fruit, be fruitful, a phrase Ela Shadday repeats with each re-naming.

Also from *Ephrathah*, *aphah*, Strong's Hebrew 644, "baker,"

Biblehub: https://biblehub.com/hebrew/644.htm

[68] *migdal-eder*: Strong's Hebrew, Biblehub, https://biblehub.com/hebrew/4029.htm

[69] *sar*: Strong's Hebrew 8269, Biblehub, https://biblehub.com/hebrew/8269.htm: defined: chief, ruler, prince. *SaR*=iSh/isha oR, "man/woman light."

[70] *sar aphah*: Strong's Hebrew 644, Biblehub, https://biblehub.com/hebrew/644.htm

[71] *epher*, Strong's Hebrew 666, Biblehub: https://biblehub.com/hebrew/666.htm

[72] *aphah*, Strong's Hebrew 644, Biblehub: https://biblehub.com/hebrew/644.htm

[73] English Standard Version of Gen 40:23: "Yet the chief cupbearer did not remember Joseph, but forgot him."

[74] *meseq*, Strong's Hebrew 4943, defined as "acquisition, possession, heir"; trans. "steward."

Biblehub: https://biblehub.com/hebrew/meshek_4943.htm

[75] "Heir" of "Father Womb," (*Ab RaHaM*); *RaHeL* passes this inheritance to Joseph.

[76] "Houses of Hillel and Shammai," Wikipedia: https://en.wikipedia.org/wiki/Houses_of_Hillel_and_Shammai 3

[77] "Hillel the Elder," Wikipedia: https://en.wikipedia.org/wiki/Hillel_the_Elder:

Footnote 3: Tosefta Hagigah 2:9; Sanhedrin 88b; Sotah 47b

[78] "Hillel and Shammai" - Chabad.org: https://www.chabad.org/library/ article_cdo/aid/2832622/jewish/ Hillel-and-Shammai.htm

[79] The modius is associated with Eleusinian deities and their Roman counterparts, the Ephesian Artemis and certain other forms of the goddess, Hecate, and Serapis. On some deities it represents fruitfulness. "Modius Headdress," Wikipedia: https://en.wikipedia.org/wiki/Modius_(headdress)

[80] This image sheds light on a letter Emperor Hadrian wrote to his friend Servianus circa 134 CE: "Egypt...I have found to be wholly fickle and inconsistent, and continually wafted about by every breath of fame. The worshipers of Sarapis (here) are called Christians, and those who are devoted to the god Sarapis call themselves Bishops of Christ."

[81] "Praise Goddess God; Praise Goddess God."

[82] Post-resurrection scene reconstructed from what is known of Roman festivals, i.e., Parilia, Veneralia, Megalesia, Lupercalia, Floralia, Quinquatria, Vestalia, et. al. These festivals and others honored goddesses Kybele, Ceres, Venus, Isis, and Ishtar: https://en.wikipedia.org/wiki/Roman_festivals (with a bit of intuition).

[83] Freedmen/women in Rome: Narcissus, Pallas, and Felix (Claudius); Caenis (Vespasian).

[84] "Plutarch," Wikipedia: https://en.wikipedia.org/wiki/Plutarch

[85] First proposed by David Trobisch: Trobisch, D. (2007/2008, December-January). "Who Published the New Testament?". New Inquiry, pp. 30-33.

"Polycarp," Wikipedia: https://en.wikipedia.org/wiki/Polycarp

[86] Acts of the Apostles, 7:9-10 "Because the patriarchs were jealous of Joseph, they sold him as a slave into Egypt. But LHM was with him and rescued him from all his troubles. LHM gave Joseph wisdom and enabled him to gain the goodwill of Pharaoh king of Egypt. So Pharaoh made him NZR over Egypt and all his palace." "Acts of the Apostles; Stephen's speech to the Sanhedrin," Hebrew words inserted to translation from Bible Gateway, www.biblegateway.com/passage/?search=acts%207&version=NIV

[87] "Q Source,"

Wikipedia: https://en.wikipedia.org/wiki/Q_source

[88] Chicago: Franciscan Herald Press, 1987. Open Library: https://openlibrary.org/books/OL2711927M/The_birth_of_the_Synoptic_Gospels

[89] Jean Carmignac:

Wikipedia: https://en.wikipedia.org/wiki/Jean_Carmignac

"Carmignac in 1963, during his work with the Dead Sea Scrolls, attempted to translate Mark from Greek to Hebrew for his use in a New Testament commentary based on the Dead Sea Scrolls. He expected many difficulties but unexpectedly discovered that the translation was not only easy, but seemed to point to Greek Mark as a translation from a Hebrew or Aramaic original."

[90] Plutarch; *Isis and Osiris*, "Introduction," (Loeb Classical Library, 1914, Babbit trans.), University of Chicago, Penelope; Bill Thayer. Emphasis added.

[91] "...according to *The Way*, which they call a heresy, I worship the God (Hebrew LHM) of our ancestors..." Acts 24:14.

[92] "Raban Gamaliel VI"

Wikipedia: https://en.m.wikipedia.org/wiki/Raban_Gamaliel_VI

[93] Codex Theodosianus:

Wikipedia: ttps://en.m.wikipedia.org/wiki/Codex_Theodosianus

[94] *Gamaliel* from *gama*, Strong's Hebrew 1572: "A primitive root (literally or figuratively) **to absorb** -- swallow, drink" plus *eLa eL: Gamaliel* means "God and Goddess within."

Biblehub: https://biblehub.com/hebrew/1572.htm

[95] "Gamaliel," New Advent, Kevin Knight (2017): http://www.newadvent.org/cathen/06374b.htm

[96] "Honorius" (emperor), Wikipedia: https://en.m.wikipedia.org/siki/Honorius_(emperor)

[97] "Porta Maggiore," Wikipedia: https://en.wikipedia.org/wiki/Porta_Maggiore

[98] Correction: "The Baker" was not Eurysacis but his wife, Atis-tia.

[99] John Henry Parker, *The Archaeology of Rome, Part IX*, "Tombs in and Near Rome" (Oxford: James Parker and Co; London: John Murray, Albemarle Street, 1877), 34-5. Public Domain.

[100] (Rome restores funerary relief of Eurysaces the baker 2019)

[101] "Most historians surmise that Jesus' cross was more likely to have been T-shaped, with the vertical element notched to allow executioners to tie the victim to the crossbeam, then raise it and set it securely into the top. The Tau cross, named for its resemblance to the Greek letter, has been adopted over time by various Christian orders and sects, and it probably bears a stronger resemblance to the object upon which Jesus died on than those crosses more commonly depicted in Christian art."

[102] Perseus Digital Library, Gregory R. Crain, Editor in Chief, Tufts University. Latin Word Study Tool, online.

[103] "Romulus and Remus," Wikipedia.

[104] "Tiberius Gemellus," Wikipedia:
https://en.wikipedia.org/wiki/Tiberius_Gemellus

[105] Wildfang, 2006, 1-31.

[106] Robert Burn, Old Rome: (London: George Bell and Sons; Cambridge: Deighton, Bell & Co., 1880), 81. Current location: Baths of Diocletian. Corpus inscriptorum latinarum, 1.2, 1206. Photograph by Jastrow, 2006.

[107] Julius and Tiberius were honored as "gods"; therefore, "...you must not think that any of these tales actually happened in the manner in which they are related." They are puzzles that must be solved.

[108] "Ides of March":

Wikipedia: https://en.wikipedia.org/wiki/Ides_of_March

[109] Gen 40:23, Hillel's Essene translation, see Part I.

[110] "Theia":

Wikipedia: https://en.wikipedia.org/wiki/Theia

[111] "Athena Promachos":

Wikipedia: https://en.wikipedia.org/wiki/Athena_Promachos: "Athena Promachos stood overlooking her city for approximately 1000 years, until shortly after 465 CE, when the sculpture was transported to Constantinople...Niketas Choniates documented a riot taking place in the Forum of Constantine in Constantinople in 1203 CE where a large, bronze, statue of Pallas-Athena. was destroyed by a "drunken crowd" of Crusaders which is now thought to have been the Athena Promachos."

[112] "Juba II," Wikipedia: https://en.wikipedia.org/wiki/Juba_II

[113] Hebrew, LZNDR: eLa ZuN eDeR, trans. "God's well-fed flock."

El: Strong's Hebrew 410: Biblehub:
https://biblehub.com/hebrew/410.htm

zun: Strong's Hebrew 2110, Biblehub:
https://biblehub.com/hebrew/2110.htm;

eder: Strong's Hebrew 5739,

Biblehub: https://biblehub.com/hebrew/5739.htm

114 "Alexander the Alabarch," Wikipedia: https://en.wikipedia.org/wiki/Alexander_the_Alabarch

115 Ovid uses the patronymic "Pallantias" or "Pallantis" as another name for]...[the Greek Eos ("Dawn"), who was the *sister of Selene*; Ovid apparently regarding]...[Eos as the daughter of (*or otherwise related to*) Pallas."

116 Marcus Antonius Pallas the Freedman was possibly the most powerful man during Claudius' reign. "Pallas (freedman)," Wikipedia: https://en.wikipedia.org/wiki/Pallas_(freedman)

117 "Pliny the Younger," Wikipedia: https://en.wikipedia.org/wiki/Pliny_the_Younger (c. 61 – c. 113).

118 Pliny the Younger letters VI To Montanus,

119 Pliny the Younger, *The Letters of Pliny the Consul with Occasional Remarks*, William Melmoth, Esq, ed. (Edinburgh: 1807) 2.8.6 (85). Emphasis added.

120 Hedrick, Charles, *Unlocking the Secrets of the Gospel According to Thomas*. (Eugene: Cascade Books, 2010), 186. Emphasis added.

121 Tacitus, *Annals; The Works* (1864-1877), (Sacred Texts Online 13.23).

122 Polycarp was burned at the stake, probably for exposing Mark's remake of *Joseph's Triumph* as the basis for *Jesus' Crucifixion* to save His Mother and to redeem women The Romans are blamed, but burning at the stake was exclusively the Church's penalty before 400. "Polycarp," Wikipedia: https://en.wikipedia.org/wiki/Polycarp

123 "Augustus and Imperial Cult," Ebrary: https://ebrary.net/140782/history/augustus_imperial_cult

124 "...you must not think that any of these tales actually happened in the manner in which they are related."

125 Marcus Aemilius Lepidus (executed by Caligula) - Wikipedia

[126] Reports accepted as "history" claim Caligula was assassinated, but abundant enigmas reveal he was merely removed from his role as Emperor which this Cameo celebrates.

[127] "Alexander the Alabarch": Wikipedia: https://en.wikipedia.org/wiki/Alexander_the_Alabarch

[128] "One of the Oldest Insults: The Origin of the Middle finger," Storypick: https://www.storypick.com/middle-finger-origins/

[128] Bruce M. Metzger and Roland E. Murphy, eds. (New York: Oxford University Press, 1994), *The New Oxford Annotated Bible with the Apocrypha: New Revised Standard Version.*

Made in United States
Orlando, FL
12 August 2024